Olly learns a lesson with Pancakes

Obedience is doing what you are told,
when you are told and with a good attitude.

Suzana N.A.A. Amo-Mensah

AuthorHouse™ UK
1663 Liberty Drive
Bloomington, IN 47403 USA
www.authorhouse.co.uk
UK TFN: 0800 0148641 (Toll Free inside the UK)
UK Local: 02036 956322 (+44 20 3695 6322 from outside the UK)

This book is printed on acid-free paper.

ISBN: 978-1-7283-7644-8 (sc)
ISBN: 978-1-7283-7645-5 (e)

Print information available on the last page.

Published by AuthorHouse

Rev. Date: 11/22/2022

authorHOUSE®

Olly learns a lesson with Pancakes

It's mid-day on a Saturday at the Peterson's residence.

Mrs. Peterson sat in her favorite rocking chair in their living room. She was knitting a sweater and enjoying some music from the 80s. Olly was Mrs Peterson's first child. She was in her room playing with her toys. Olly was four years old.

Mrs. Peterson got up to go and check on Olly. Olly has been quiet for more than 20 minutes which was quite unusual. She must be up to something! Mrs. Peterson thought.

And oh! she wasn't wrong. Olly was happily playing with her toys and had scattered them in the room.

Mrs. Peterson said to Olly, "I see you've been busy, Sweetheart".

Olly smiled at her mum and responded, "Yes, mummy. I am having a fun playtime with my toys".

Mummy, can you make me some pancakes today, please? Olly asked her mummy.

She loves pancakes very much. Olly wants mummy to prepare some pancakes for snack.

Mummy has been teaching Olly how to earn what she wants for weeks now.

So she said to Olly, "I will make you yummy pancakes and add some vanilla ice cream,

but you have to work for it, ok?"

Olly asked mummy, "how do I do that, mum?"

"You must first pick up all your scattered toys into the toy bag", mummy answered.

Olly did not like the idea of picking up all the toys because there were many toys scattered on the floor in her room.

She made an angry face, folded her arms and started to cry.

Mummy walked to Olly, sat next to her and wrapped her arms around her.

She said softly to Olly, "Olly, picking up your toys is not a punishment".

"You must learn to be organized. Don't you want your room to be clean and cozy? A clean, cozy room makes you sleep well", mummy said to Olly.

"When you are done playing with your toys, you need to put them back just how you found them. If you start now, you will be done in no time".

Olly responded, "but there are so many toys, mummy".

Mum replied, "that is why you should choose the toys you would like to play with".

If you pick up your toys like mummy wants you to do, mummy will make you very delicious pancakes. We can make them together, and I will get you your favorite vanilla ice cream.

Olly's face lit up. She jumped up, wiped her tears and gave mummy a big hug.

Olly started collecting each toy and putting them into the toy bag. After 5 minutes, she was done.

Mummy gave Olly a big hug and said to her. "Well done! So you see, it was not difficult picking up your toys after all. Look how clean and cozy your room looks".

Olly took a step back, and with her head down, she said to her mum, "I am sorry mummy, for being naughty when you first asked me to pick up my toys. Can you please forgive me?"

Mummy smiled and said, "I forgive you, sweetheart. You have earned some yummy pancakes for picking up your toys".

Now let's go and make pancakes! The two headed for the kitchen.

9

In the kitchen, mummy handed Olly an apron. Olly looked confused. She did not know how to wear an apron. She asked mummy, "mummy, how do I wear this?"

Mummy smiled and replied: "You wear it over your dress, so you do not get dirty while cooking. Come, let me help you put it on". Olly was so excited. She was beaming with smiles. She said to mummy, "yay! This is so exciting. I am a chef"!

Mummy and Olly both laughed. Then mummy said to Olly, "these are the ingredients and things you will need. A bowl, sugar, flour, eggs, milk, a pinch of salt, nutmeg, wooden spatula, oil, and fry pan".

First of all, Chef Olly, mummy said smiling; "you whisk together the flour, sugar, a pinch of salt and nutmeg". Mummy measured a cup of flour, a half cup of sugar, a pinch of salt and a teaspoon of nutmeg into a plastic blow. She gave the whisk to Olly and said to her, "whisk this, Olly".

Olly began to mix with her tender hands and splashed flour onto her face in the process. They both laughed out. Mummy took Olly to the sink to rinse her face. Just when she wiped Olly's face clean, Olly's favorite song was being played on the radio in the kitchen.

"I've got sunshine on a cloudy day.
When it's cold outside
I've got the month of May
I guess you'd say
What can make me feel this way
My girl, my girl, my girl
Talkin' 'bout my girl
My girl"

She exclaimed, "Mummy! That is my song! The Temptations"!

Olly started singing along, and dancing and mummy joined her. Daddy often played this song for Olly and danced with her. It was their daddy-daughter dance song.

Olly was having a great day!

Mummy moved to the kitchen table. She said to Olly, "come here, hunny, let us finish making the pancakes before Reuben wakes up". Reuben is Olly's little brother. He is a year and 6months old. He was having a play time with daddy when he fell asleep.

Mummy took a Pyrex measuring cup and poured some milk, melted butter and one egg. She said to Olly, "Olly, I will whisk this mix together with the flour and other ingredients in the bowl, ok". Remember it is teamwork, ok! You can achieve your goals faster when you work together as a team.

Mummy whisked and whisked the mixture until she got the batter she wanted. Then she took the pancake pan and put it on the oven to heat it up.

Olly watched on. Then she said, mummy, "can we use your cookie cutter to make shapes with the pancakes?" Mummy's face lit up. "Yes, we can, hunny. But first, I will fetch the batter with a ladle and spread it into the greased pancake pan; then, I will use the spatula to turn it when it is cooked on one end so that it can cook on the other end as well. We can try cutting one with the cookie-cutter, okay?" "Ok, mum", Olly responded.

Just when mummy was about to fry the last pancake, daddy walked into the kitchen with Reuben.

He said, "hmm...I love the aroma in here. You two have been busy. What are you making, Olly? I can see you are a chef today". They all laughed. Daddy put Reuben into his high seat and handed him a juice in his feeding bottle.

He said to mum, let me help you set the table for lunch. Daddy set the table with the help of Olly as mummy cleaned up the kitchen. He taught Olly how to place the fork and knife properly. "Fork on your left, knife on your right," daddy kept repeating.

FAMILY TIME IS THE BEST TIME

19

The family sat together and had a good lunch, of course, some pancakes with vanilla ice cream as dessert. They talked about how the morning went. Olly told daddy how she earned her pancakes. She loved how mummy involved her in the making of the pancakes and enjoyed the dance time. Olly went on and on about how good her day had been. Daddy asked Olly, "Olly hunny, what lesson have you learnt this afternoon?"

Olly replied, "hmm...I learnt how to pick up my toys after playing so that I could have a clean, cozy room. I also learnt that if I do what mummy asks me to do, I will earn pancakes". And with that, they all laughed.

Olly stretched while yawning. "I feel tired now. I want to take a nap, mummy. It has been a fun afternoon. Thank you, mummy, thank you, daddy!"

And with that, Olly excused herself and tucked herself into bed in her clean, cozy room.

The End

Ingram Content Group UK Ltd.
Milton Keynes UK
UKHW050346090323
418282UK00002B/81